The Wayland Library of Science and Technology

AIR AND OCEANS

DOUGAL DIXON

Wayland

The Wayland Library of Science and Technology

The Nature of Matter
The Universal Forces
Stars and Galaxies
The Solar System
The Changing Landscape
Air and Oceans
Origins of Life
The Science of Life
Plants and Animals
Animal Behaviour
The Human Machine
Health and Medicine

The Environment
Feeding the World
Raw Materials
Manufacturing Industry
Energy Sources
The Power Generators
Transport
Space Travel
Communications
The Computer Age
Scientific Instruments
Towards Tomorrow

Advisory Series Editor
Robin Kerrod

Consultants
Professor D.C. Imrie, Dr J. Beynon

Editor: Steve Luck
Designer: David West · Children's Book Design
Production: Steve Elliott
Art Director: John Ridgeway
Project Director: Lawrence Clarke

First published in 1990 by
Wayland (Publishers) Ltd
61 Western Road, Hove
East Sussex BN3 1JD, England

AN EQUINOX BOOK

Planned and produced by:
Equinox (Oxford) Limited
Musterlin House, Jordan Hill Road,
Oxford OX2 8DP

British Library Cataloguing in Publication Data
Dixon, Dougal
Air and Oceans
1. Oceans: 2. Weather
I. Title
551.46
551.5
ISBN 1-85210-889-4

Media conversion and typesetting by Peter
MacDonald, Una Macnamara and Vanessa Hersey
Origination by Hong Kong Reprohouse Co Ltd
Printed in Italy by Rotolito Lombarda
S.p.A., Milan
Bound in France by AGM

Front cover: Waves lapping on a beach.
Back cover: The global pattern of the wind.

Contents

Introduction

Earth is the only planet in the Solar System that supports life. And the key to life on Earth is water. All living things, plants and animals alike, require water for their body structures and for making or digesting their food.

Water exists as a liquid in vast quantities in the oceans, rivers and lakes. It occurs as solid ice at the North and South Poles. It is also present in small amounts as water vapour in the atmosphere. Water moves between the surface and the atmosphere in a never-ending cycle.

The shifting around the world of air masses containing more or less moisture is one of the major factors that determines the weather. The average weather pattern, or climate, at a particular place depends on many other factors besides. One of the most important of these is the temperature.

◀ Water is found in lakes, rivers and oceans. Snow and ice are forms of frozen water. Clouds are droplets of water; the atmosphere also holds water as water vapour. All plants and animals need water to live.

The oceans

Spot facts

- *The oceans have a total area of 361,300,000 square kilometres. This represents 71 per cent of the total surface area of the Earth.*

- *The total volume of the oceans is 1,349,929,000 cubic kilometres.*

- *The deepest point is in the Marianas Trench, 11,033 m deep.*

- *Traces of all the chemical elements are found in the oceans, including 60,000 tonnes of gold.*

- *If removed from the sea, the dissolved salt would cover the land to a depth of more than 150 m.*

We call our planet the Earth. It would be more appropriate if we called it the Water, because more than two-thirds of its area is covered by the seas and oceans. This is well brought out in satellite photographs and the views that astronauts have from space. The overall colour is blue, caused both by the effect of the atmosphere and by the vast areas of water beneath. It is the presence of all this water that has made life possible. All life processes involve water, and life evolved in the sea about 3,500 million years ago, and only about 500 million years ago did life move on to land.

► The constant movement of the ocean is seen in the pounding surf of the shoreline. The wind moves the waves. On a larger scale the winds and the Sun create the great ocean currents. The gravity of the Moon and Sun gives rise to the tides.

The waters

The water in the sea tastes very salty. Drinking it is likely to make you sick. Seawater is not pure, but contains a large quantity of salts that have been dissolved from the rocks of the Earth's crust. The actual salinity, or saltiness, varies from place to place. It is saltiest in warm enclosed seas, where water is constantly being evaporated. It is least salty in the cold northern and southern oceans, where it is diluted by rain and melting ice. It is also less salty where great rivers like the Amazon or Niger flow into the ocean. However, the proportions of the different salts present are constant throughout the world.

The temperature of seawater varies a great deal over the surface of the ocean, but the temperature beneath is fairly constant. The slightest variation in temperature can trigger ocean currents.

Combinations of salinity, temperature, currents and other factors determine the amount of life present in any ocean region. Vigorous life is confined to the surface and a few hundred metres below it. There the Sun shines into the water and plant life, some of it microscopic, can grow. Small invertebrates feed on the plants, and fish feed on these. A whole ecosystem is supported. In the dark depths the Sun has never shone. The only life consists of creatures that feed on dead organic debris, which rains down from the more fertile layers above, or that prey on one another.

▼ The distribution of land and sea on our globe is not even. Most of the ocean area lies as the Pacific on one side. This is an accident of plate tectonics. 200 million years ago the inequality was even greater, with all the continents fused together and the rest of the world covered with a single ocean called Panthalassa.

Seawater composition

Much of the gas belched out of volcanoes is water vapour. It is actually recycled seawater, which has been carried down into the depths of the crust by plate tectonic movement. The salinity of ocean water varies usually between 33 and 38 parts per thousand. The dissolved salts contain nearly all the chemical elements. The commonest are sodium and chlorine, which together make up common salt.

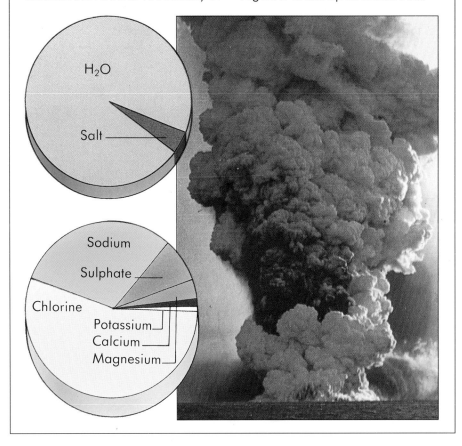

H₂O

Salt

Sodium

Sulphate

Chlorine

Potassium
Calcium
Magnesium

The ocean surface

The continents are large islands, mostly quite separate from each other. As a result, the oceans form a single continuous body of water. In some places, such as the Bering Strait, the gaps between the continents are narrow; in others, such as the East Indies, they are choked with islands. But nowhere is there an area of ocean that is completely isolated from any other. Political problems aside, we can sail from a port on one continent to any other seaport in the world. For convenience, however, we often talk about the seven seas. These are the North Atlantic, South Atlantic, Indian, North Pacific, South Pacific, Arctic and Antarctic Oceans.

The surface of this vast waterway is constantly in motion, notably through the movements of ocean currents. Vertical currents are set up by convection. This happens because a cold mass of fluid is denser than a warmer mass of the same fluid and sinks through it. Cold water from melted ice at the North Pole sinks through the surrounding warmer water. It then travels for thousands of kilometres as an undersea current along the bed of the Atlantic. On the surface, however, it tends to be the prevailing winds that power the ocean currents. The Trade Winds are those that blow towards the Equator from the north-east and south-east. The surface waters blown by them produce an overall westward flow of equatorial water as the equatorial currents.

When this water reaches a continent, it sweeps north and south, producing warm currents along the east coast of that continent. The Gulf Stream in the North Atlantic, the Kuro Shio in the North Pacific and the Australian Current in the South Pacific are examples. The movement is completed when the water sweeps towards the Equator along the eastern edge of the ocean and joins up with the beginnings of the equatorial currents. These include the Californian Current and the Peru Current in the eastern Pacific Ocean.

Hence, the world pattern of ocean currents is based on a vast system of circular movements, or gyres, each occupying half an ocean. The movement of warm currents along cold continental edges, and cold currents along warm continental edges, helps to modify the climates in these coastal areas.

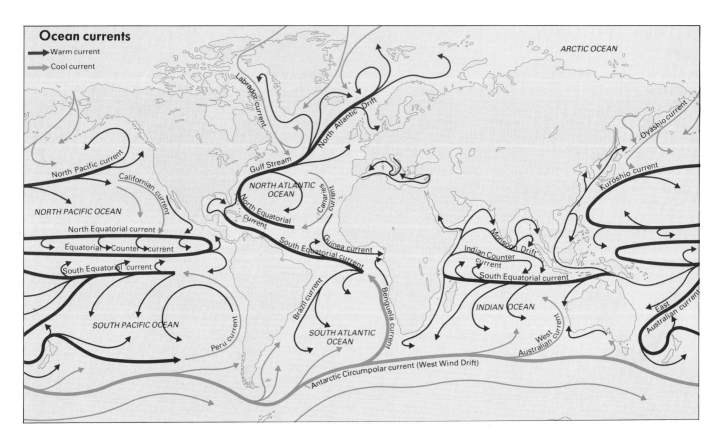

▲ Penguins and flat-topped icebergs typify the cold Antarctic Ocean. The icebergs are made from glaciers that have flowed seawards off the edge of Antarctica. The ice at the North Pole, on the other hand, is formed on the sea's surface.

◄ Prevailing winds drive the ocean currents. The Westerlies blowing in the far south produce the cold circumpolar current called the West Wind Drift. This separates the Antarctic from warmer waters farther north and keeps Antarctica frozen. Elsewhere, the ocean gyres bring warm or cool currents to the edges of the continents.

► During the ice ages of the last 2 million years the sea level changed. So much water was locked up in the expanded ice cap at the North Pole that the volume of liquid water left was less than it is now and the sea level was lower. Land appeared where there is now shallow sea. At the same time in the far north, the great weight of the ice on the land pushed the land downwards, and sea levels were higher than they are today. The ice came and went several times, and we can often see the different sea levels as "raised beaches". These are banks a few metres above sea level that mark the ancient shorelines.

Today

An ice age

The ocean floor

Under the sea is a varied landscape that is rarely seen by human beings. It is a landscape of mountains, volcanoes and broad, flat plains. Only since the 1960s have we really begun to understand it.

There are a number of different zones of the ocean floor. First there is the continental shelf. This is merely the edge of the continent that is awash. If we drill through the sediment on the continental shelf, we find continental crust beneath it, not oceanic crust. The continental shelf can be hundreds of kilometres broad where it is at the edge of an old continent, as for example in the North Sea and Hudson Bay. But the shelf is very narrow or non-existent where new mountain ranges are being pushed up along a coastline, as along the western coast of South America.

At the edge of the continental shelf the seabed slopes downwards into the depths. This feature is known as the continental slope, and it marks the edge of the continent itself. In some places – usually offshore from the mouths of large rivers – the continental slope is cut by vast canyons, wider and deeper than any canyon on land. These have been eroded out by debris swept down from the rivers.

At the foot of the continental slope lies the continental rise. This is not as steep as the

▼ Coral reefs are found only in shallow tropical waters. Coral builds out from an island in a shelf called a fringing reef. Over thousands of years the island may sink as the coral builds up. A lagoon then separates the reef, now a barrier reef, from the dwindling island. When the island sinks completely, it forms an atoll, which is a ring of coral surrounding a lagoon.

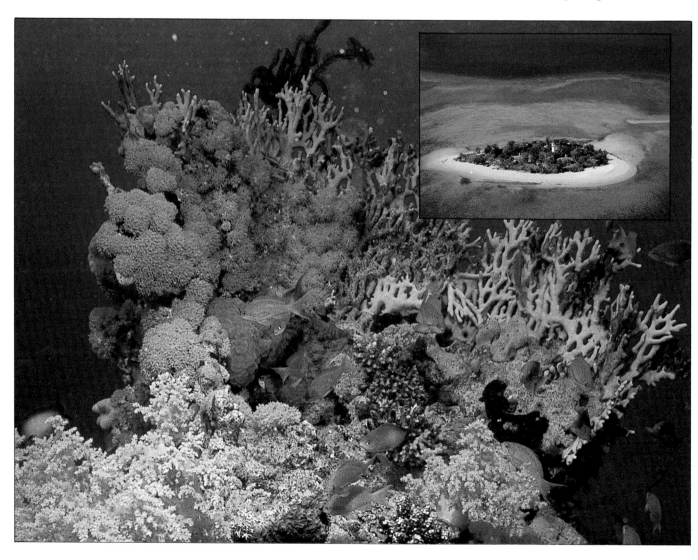

continental slope itself and is built up from debris that has been brought down from the continental shelf above. Perhaps the largest are the fans of material that spread out through the northern Indian Ocean from the outflowings of the rivers Ganges and Indus.

The abyssal plain is the floor of the ocean itself. With true oceanic crust as its foundation, it extends between the continents. It is covered with a fine muddy deposit called ooze. This is made up of the remains of millions of sea creatures that have settled on the dark bottom over many millions of years. There is no debris from the land here. Across the abyssal plain rise the volcanic ocean ridges. Occasionally the plain drops away into the ocean trenches, the deepest points of the ocean, where the old crust is continually being destroyed.

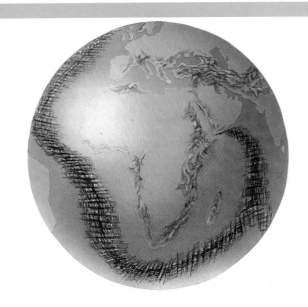

▲ The ocean ridges are the most extensive geographical feature on the Earth. They run through the beds of all the oceans without a break.

Geography of the ocean floor

The continental shelf consists of continental crust and reaches out from the shore to a depth of about 150 m. At its outer edge it drops away as the continental slope, with a gradient of between 3 and 20 degrees. The slope, and the continental rise at the bottom, gives out on to the abyssal plain at a depth of about 4,000 m. Ocean ridges rise from the abyssal plain to heights of between 500 and 1,000 m. Volcanoes are constantly erupting in the rift valley that exists along its crest. The ridge volcanoes may occasionally reach the ocean surface, but more often they are completely submerged. Seamounts on the abyssal plain, some with flat eroded tops, are the remains of these volcanoes. The ocean trenches, in which one part of the Earth's crust is being swallowed up beneath another, are the deepest points on Earth.

▼ The volcanic activity in an ocean ridge is dramatically shown by the presence of "smokers". These are jets of hot water that burst from the Earth's crust at great depths. The "smoke" is caused by fine particles of minerals in the water.

The ocean floor

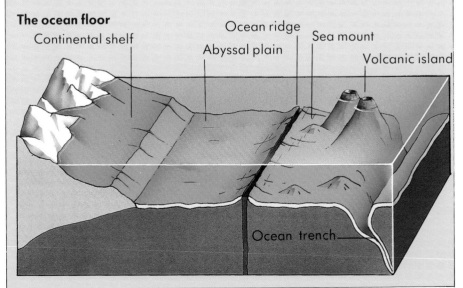

Continental shelf
Ocean ridge
Abyssal plain
Sea mount
Volcanic island
Ocean trench

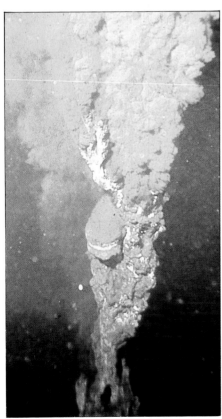

Cycling the water

▶ Liquid water, cascading down a waterfall, in a lake or in the oceans, is what makes our planet unique in the Solar System. Without it life would be impossible, because all the biological and chemical reactions that sustain life can take place only in the presence of water.

More than two-thirds of the Earth's surface is covered with water. By far the greatest volume of this – 97.2 per cent – is contained in the oceans. The remainder is found as water vapour, fresh water and ice. Water occurs as vapour in the atmosphere, as ice in the glaciers and ice caps, and as liquid water flowing in rivers, standing in lakes and swamps, and absorbed into rocks and soil as groundwater. Water vapour in the atmosphere condenses to form raindrops, which fall to the ground. Rainwater collects to form streams and rivers, which flow to the sea. If it were not for water, which is available in most places on the Earth, life would be impossible on our planet.

Moving water

Physical conditions on the Earth's surface ensure that water can exist in all three of its possible states. It can exist as a gas – as water vapour; it can exist as a liquid – in the form that we most often see it; or it can exist as a solid – in the form of ice. It takes a relatively small shift of conditions such as temperature or pressure to change water from one state to the next. One cold night can turn a liquid pond into solid ice, or one hot day can evaporate a large puddle to vapour, leaving the surface dry.

Water is continually evaporating into the atmosphere from open bodies of water, such as seas and lakes. Then it condenses and falls as rain. The rain that falls on the land runs off the surface or sinks into the rocks and soil to form the groundwater. It re-emerges at springs and forms the beginnings of streams and rivers, and flows back to the lakes and oceans. This whole process is known as the water cycle.

The cycle has many side branches as well. Water that falls on the ground may evaporate straight away. Groundwater is drawn up through plants and evaporated from leaves.

The water cycle

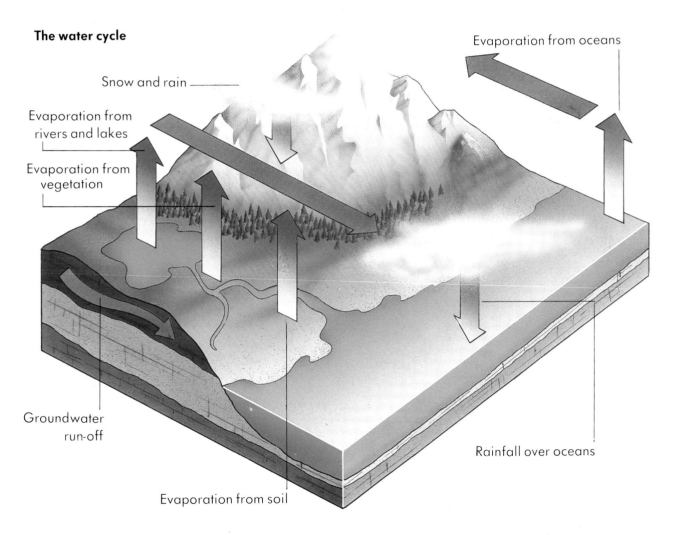

Snow and rain

Evaporation from oceans

Evaporation from rivers and lakes

Evaporation from vegetation

Groundwater run-off

Evaporation from soil

Rainfall over oceans

▲ Water goes round and round in the water cycle. The main upward movement is by evaporation. Water evaporated as vapour from oceans, rivers and lakes passes into the atmosphere. Some water vapour is also "breathed out" by plants. High in the air, water vapour condenses to form clouds. Sideways movement occurs when clouds are blown along by the wind. Finally, downward movement, to complete the cycle, takes place when it rains. When it is cold, rain falls as snowflakes or hailstones, and lies as snow and ice. Sometimes snow and ice can even change directly into vapour without passing through a liquid phase.

Water resources

We all need water to keep us alive. Each of us needs at least 2 litres every day just to keep the body working. In Westernized societies the daily consumption increases because of the water used for washing and the demands of industry and agriculture. On average it takes about 2,000 litres of water a day to support one person in an industrial nation. It is no wonder that water is regarded as one of the most valuable of the Earth's resources.

The Earth's surface is largely covered by water, but unfortunately most of this is unusable or in the wrong place. Many rapidly expanding centres of population lie in areas where there is very little water because the climate is too dry and the rainfall irregular. Other expanding centres of population lie where the presence of water is an embarrassment, such as by tropical rivers that are likely to flood and promote the spread of disease.

Much of the usable water is obtained from rivers. The irregular or seasonal flow of a river can be regulated and controlled by using dams.

Built across the flow of a river, a dam traps the water and fills the valley behind it to produce a reservoir. The larger a dam becomes, however, the more problems are associated with it. A heavy structure on unstable ground could collapse, and with several million tonnes of water behind it the result would be disastrous. Reservoirs may also silt up, because the original flow of the river is disrupted. The floor of the reservoir builds up so that it becomes shallow and can hold only a small fraction of the original water. The stagnant surface of the water may also promote the growth of water weed that both chokes waterways and makes the water unmanageable.

The other great water source is groundwater,

▶ The Kariba Dam, at the border between Zambia and Zimbabwe, in southern Africa. The dam creates the large reservoir of water called Lake Kariba.

▼ The plain of the River Indus in India is irrigated by a complex system of channels that bring the spring meltwater from Himalayan glaciers to the fields.

the water that has soaked into the rocks and soils of an area. This can be extracted by digging wells or boreholes and installing pumps. In the driest areas, however, this does not represent an inexhaustible supply. Much of the water that is being pumped up in northern Africa is actually rain that fell in the Ice Age. Once that has gone, there will be no more.

As the world population grows there will be bigger and more elaborate schemes for distributing water to where it is needed. Each will bring its own problems.

▶ The constant cycling of water is well seen in the daily downpours that occur in the areas of tropical forest that straddle the Equator.

Groundwater

Springs, wells and oases

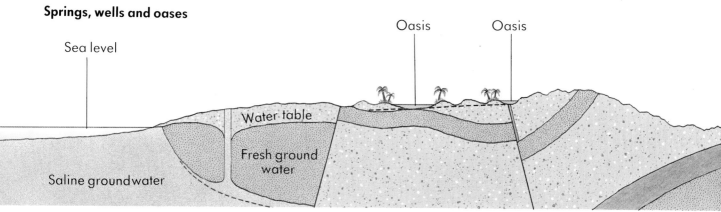

Sea level

Oasis Oasis

Water table

Fresh ground water

Saline groundwater

When rain falls on the soil, some of it washes off as surface flow. The remainder sinks into the soil and becomes groundwater.

Soils tend to be quite loose and have large air spaces and pockets between the particles. These are easily filled up with water, in a similar way to the holes in a sponge. The rocks beneath are more compact, but usually contain air pores as well. If the pores are connected together, water can soak through. We say that the rock is permeable. At some distance below the surface the rocks are so compact that they have no spaces in them and water cannot penetrate. The rock is impermeable. When the rock above this level is full of water, it is said to be saturated. Above the saturated zone is a region in which the water is seeping downwards. This is the zone of intermittent saturation.

The upper boundary of the saturated zone is called the water table. Its level varies from time to time, being higher in wet weather and very low in times of drought. When wells are drilled, they are driven down to below the water table. Water from the surrounding rocks gathers in the bottom of the hole. Where the water table reaches the surface, the water leaks out and becomes a spring. Other springs form when the water from the saturated zone seeps upwards through cracks or faults.

The movement of water through underground rocks is slow, usually taking years. Once underground, the water is protected from evaporation, and its passage through the pores of the rocks filters it so that it is usually quite clean. Accordingly, underground water is a valuable resource, although there may be some salts and minerals dissolved in it.

It is estimated that about 62.5 per cent of the world's fresh water is present in the form of groundwater in the rocks.

◄ Groundwater is widely exploited in areas where there is little rainfall and few rivers. In desert oases, such as this one at Taghit in Algeria, the water table reaches the surface and a freshwater lake forms. The water is used for drinking and irrigation.

► In most instances the water table lies well below the surface, and the water has to be brought up by artificial means. Here oxen are used to turn a wooden gear that brings water to the surface by a bucket wheel for distribution to the groves of date palms. Desert peoples have become skilful at drawing water and transporting it to the fields by irrigation systems.

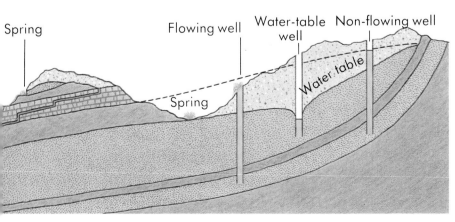

Spring   Flowing well   Water-table well   Non-flowing well

Spring

Water table

◄ A rock that contains groundwater is called an aquifer. Different kinds of wells can be drilled to reach water in an aquifer. A particular type is the artesian. Exposed rocks absorb water in a hilly area. In the nearby lowlands a well drilled through the overlying impermeable bed into the aquifer reaches the water. The pressure of the water coming down the slope of the aquifer pushes the water up the borehole until it gushes out at the surface.

Clouds and rain

The water vapour in the atmosphere makes up only about 0.001 per cent of the total water supply of the world. But without it all life would be confined to the sea. The proportions of most of the gases in the atmosphere are constant wherever we go, but the proportion of water vapour varies.

The concentration of vapour in the atmosphere depends largely on the temperature and pressure. When the atmosphere is holding as much vapour as it can at a particular temperature and pressure, it is said to be saturated. Any change to these conditions will turn some of the vapour back to liquid. Because the atmosphere is always in motion, the physical conditions are changing all the time. So is the amount of water in the air.

Such changes can be caused by the wind blowing from a warm region to a cold region. Convection currents may lift warm air up to heights where the pressure is less. Wind blowing off the sea can carry moisture up a hillside, where the air becomes cooler as it rises. When these things happen, the vapour in the air turns to water in the form of tiny droplets. These are too light to fall to the ground and remain suspended as clouds.

Different types of clouds form under different conditions. At very great heights, above about 7,000 m, the conditions produce clouds of ice crystals rather than droplets. At other heights the water droplets form layer clouds, called stratus; or heaped clouds, called cumulus; or a combination of the two. Thunderclouds have such strong convection currents that the main cloud mass is made of water droplets, while its crown is of ice.

Cooling and decreasing the pressure still further causes the droplets to mass together into larger drops, and these fall as rain.

▼ A satellite view of a hurricane. The rapid heating of surface ocean waters in tropical regions causes hurricanes to form. Turbulent and constantly changing conditions are found in the hurricane. Winds spiral in towards a low-pressure area and thick banks of clouds form as the pressure becomes less and less. Torrential rains fall as the pressure reduces still further.

▶ Thunderstorms develop where a patch of air heats up quickly and rises. Raindrops form under the reduced pressure at height, and are carried up and down by the strong currents. The growing drops become too big to be stable and split into smaller drops, producing an electrical discharge. A strong charge builds up in the cloud and flashes to earth as lightning.

▲ Heavy seasonal rains called monsoons develop around the north of the Indian Ocean. In the winter the Asian landmass cools and dry air flows seawards. In the summer the continent heats up and draws in wet air from the ocean. The moisture falls as rain over the land.

▼ Snow is frozen water. At certain temperatures the vapour in the atmosphere does not form water droplets, but forms ice crystals instead. When the crystals clump together and fall to the ground, the result is snow. When raindrops freeze, they fall as hail.

Life-giving atmosphere

Spot facts

- The atmosphere weighs about 5,000 million million tonnes.

- At sea level, the weight of the atmosphere exerts a pressure of 1.05 kg on every square centimetre.

- We can study the change in climate over the last half million years by looking at the composition of the ancient ice in Antarctica and Greenland.

- The greenhouse effect may help to avert another ice age.

The Earth's atmosphere is an ocean of air that surrounds the planet. Air is a mixture of gases, mainly nitrogen and oxygen. We cannot see it, or taste it or smell it, yet air is vital for life. Layers of gases high in the atmosphere shield us from harmful radiation from the Sun. But the increasing destruction of these protective layers caused by pollution is altering the Earth's climate. We take oxygen from air into our bodies with every breath, and without it we suffocate. Oxygen in the air is also needed for fuels to burn. And air does have substance. Without it, birds and aircraft could not fly.

► This beautiful sunset was caused by dust in the lower atmosphere. Dust scatters blue light, but lets red light pass through.

The air we breathe

The atmosphere is a thin layer of air that surrounds our planet. On a small model of the Earth its thickness would be hardly noticeable – no thicker in than the skin of an apple. But its weight at ground level gives us the air pressure under which we and all other land-living creatures evolved. The higher up we go, the thinner the atmosphere becomes. At a height of several hundred kilometres it fades away into the vacuum of space.

The atmosphere is a mixture of gases. The main gases are nitrogen and oxygen, with about four parts of nitrogen to every one of oxygen. The remainder – just over one per cent of the whole – consists of carbon dioxide and rare gases like argon, helium and neon. These rare gases are called noble or inert gases because they do not take part in chemical reactions. The proportions of all these gases tend to remain the same all the time.

▶ Most of the atmosphere consists of nitrogen, but about 21 per cent of it is oxygen generated by the action of plant life. The oxygen makes Earth's atmosphere different from those of other planets.

▼ Mountaineers who climb to high altitudes have to carry a supply of oxygen to breathe. At high altitudes the air pressure is less, and so there is less oxygen available in the air.

There are, however, a few variable components in the atmosphere. The most important variable is water vapour. It can be almost absent in desert areas but can reach a concentration of about three per cent in very humid regions. The presence of water vapour is essential to life. Sulphur dioxide is another variable. This is not essential to life, and can in fact be quite harmful. It is produced in large amounts by volcanoes and by burning fuels such as coal and oil.

At a height of between 15 and 50 km there is the so-called ozone layer. Ozone is a type of oxygen. High-energy ultraviolet radiation from the Sun affects oxygen in the layer and turns it into ozone. This reaction absorbs ultraviolet radiation and prevents most of it from reaching the Earth's surface. The layer is important because too much ultraviolet radiation would be harmful to living things.

Composition of air

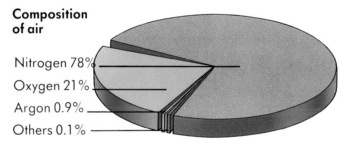

Nitrogen 78%
Oxygen 21%
Argon 0.9%
Others 0.1%

The atmosphere's structure

The layers of air that form the atmosphere stretch upwards above our heads for about 700 km. At that height the air is extremely thin. At even higher altitudes the atmosphere fades away into the airless vacuum of space.

The "thickness" of the atmosphere is called its density. Air is densest near the surface of the Earth. It is less dense at the tops of tall mountains. Atmospheric pressure is also greatest near the ground. The pressure is caused by the weight of layers of air pressing down from above.

The atmosphere can be divided into a number of layers, each with its own properties. The lowermost 11 km or so is called the troposphere. Although it is quite a thin layer, the troposphere contains, under pressure, the greatest proportion of air by mass. All the physical activities that affect the weather take place in this region.

The top of the troposphere is a theoretical boundary called the tropopause. Above this lies the stratosphere, extending up to about 50 km. Most military and long-distance aircraft operate in this region. The ozone layer, within this region, absorbs much of the Sun's energy. As a result, the temperature is quite high in the stratosphere.

Above the stratopause – the upper limit of the stratosphere – stretches the mesosphere, up to about 80 km. The temperature there is low and the air is thin. But it is still thick enough for meteorites to burn up as they pass through it.

Beyond its upper boundary, the mesopause, the mesosphere gives way to the thermosphere. This is a another region of high temperatures caused by absorption of solar radiation. Then comes the exosphere, which eventually fades away to nothing at about 700 km above the surface of the Earth.

▶ Layers of the atmosphere. The weight of the air pressing down on itself compresses the lower layers. As a result the lowermost layer, the troposphere, contains 80 per cent of the atmosphere by mass. But it occupies a volume of only 1.5 per cent. Above the stratosphere there is only one per cent of the mass of air, but this is spread through 93 per cent of the volume. The two diagrams (right) compare the composition of the atmosphere in terms of mass and in terms of volume.

▼ Radiation from the Sun includes light, heat rays and ultraviolet radiation. Over 30 per cent of the radiation reaching the Earth is reflected back by the atmosphere, by clouds and by the ground. Most of the remaining 70 per cent is absorbed. The ground reflects the least radiation and absorbs the most.

SOLAR RADIATION 100%

21% reflected by cloud

6% reflected by atmosphere

5% reflected by ground

15% absorbed by atmosphere

3% absorbed by cloud

50% absorbed by ground

Composition by mass

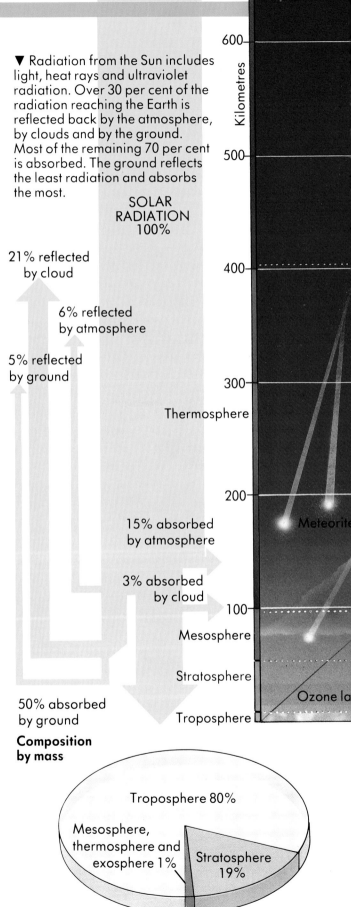

700
Exosphere

600

500

Kilometres

400

Thermosphere

300

200

Meteorite

100

Mesosphere

Stratosphere

Ozone la

Troposphere

Troposphere 80%

Mesosphere, thermosphere and exosphere 1%

Stratosphere 19%

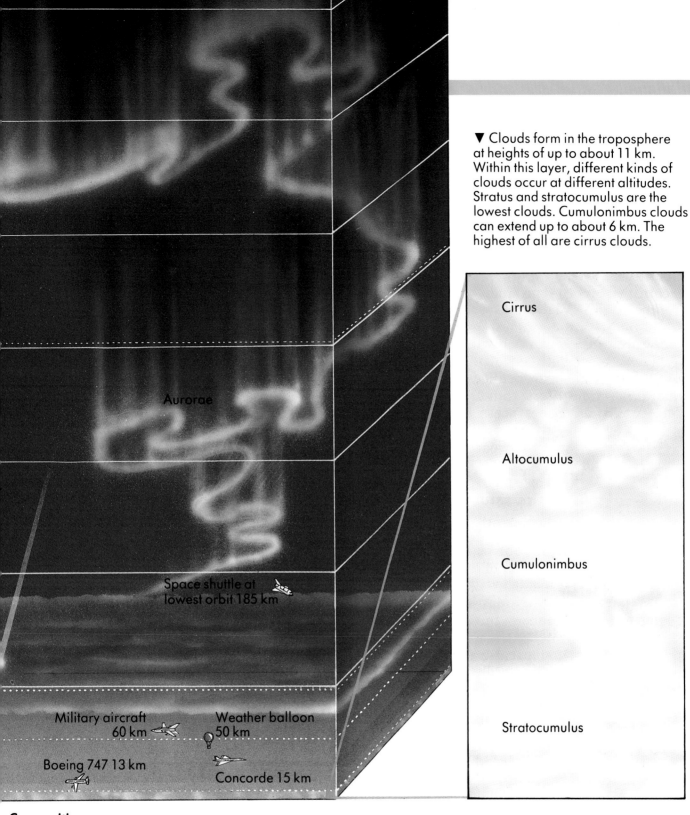

▼ Clouds form in the troposphere at heights of up to about 11 km. Within this layer, different kinds of clouds occur at different altitudes. Stratus and stratocumulus are the lowest clouds. Cumulonimbus clouds can extend up to about 6 km. The highest of all are cirrus clouds.

Cirrus

Altocumulus

Cumulonimbus

Stratocumulus

Aurorae

Space shuttle at lowest orbit 185 km

Military aircraft 60 km

Weather balloon 50 km

Boeing 747 13 km

Concorde 15 km

Composition by volume

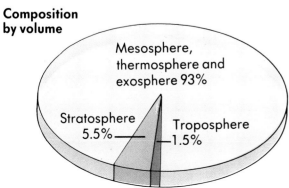

Mesosphere, thermosphere and exosphere 93%

Stratosphere 5.5%

Troposphere 1.5%

▲ The different layers of the atmosphere have different properties. The interaction between the solar wind and the Earth's magnetic field produces the light effects of the aurora in the exosphere and the thermosphere. About half of the solar radiation is absorbed or reflected by different layers before it reaches the ground. This absorption produces different temperature conditions in different layers. Meteorites burn up in the upper layers. Only the troposphere has enough oxygen to support life.

The changing atmosphere

The atmosphere that formed as the Earth first solidified was very different from the atmosphere of today. Even now it gradually continues to change.

The first atmosphere probably consisted mostly of carbon dioxide, nitrogen, hydrogen, carbon monoxide and inert gases. The strong solar wind would immediately have blasted much of this away into space. Then as the Earth began to solidify, gases were emitted from the cooling rocks and built up the next atmosphere. These gases consisted largely of carbon dioxide, with some nitrogen, hydrogen and traces of argon. Volcanoes continued to bring up water vapour, carbon dioxide, hydrogen sulphide and nitrogen. The Sun's energy broke down some of the water vapour into hydrogen and oxygen.

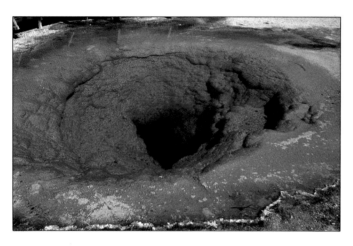

▲ This colony of green algae is living on chemicals in the hot, oxygen-free water of a hot spring. The first living things must also have lived in an oxygen-free environment. Their biochemistry was what scientists call "anaerobic".

It also converted some of the oxygen into ozone to produce an ozone layer early in Earth's history. The first oceans formed when so much water vapour was released that the atmosphere could not hold it all. The vapour condensed into clouds, and it began to rain.

The next major change in the atmosphere took place when carbon dioxide dissolved in the early oceans. We can tell that this was happening because we can find early rocks that contain calcite. This mineral was formed from carbon dioxide dissolved in sea water. The level of carbon dioxide in the atmosphere fell from about 80 per cent to its present level of about 0.05 per cent by about 1,000 million years ago. Meanwhile, the hydrogen in the atmosphere was leaking off into space. It was too light to be held firmly by the Earth's gravity. As a result of the loss of these gases, the proportion of nitrogen gradually grew until it reached its present proportion of about 80 per cent.

Enter oxygen

The most important change to the atmosphere began about 2,500 million years ago. Before this time there was very little oxygen in the atmosphere. We can tell this because of the rocks that formed at the time. The iron in them formed minerals that were poor in oxygen. But if there had been free oxygen in the atmosphere, the iron would have formed rust-red

► Colonies of aerobic bacteria. Many types of these live in stagnant lakes and estuaries. The colonies shown here are living in black mud that contain no oxygen.

▲ The burning of coal, oil and wood has an effect on the composition of the atmosphere. Burning uses up oxygen from the air and releases carbon dioxide. Water vapour is also produced by burning these fuels. Carbon dioxide and water vapour together give rise to what is known as the greenhouse effect. The Sun's rays pass through the atmosphere and warm the Earth in the normal way, but the excess heat cannot escape back out again. Sulphur dioxide is also produced by burning coal, and this reacts with the moisture in the air to produce sulphuric acid. The result is acid rain, which damages plants and poisons lakes wherever it falls.

minerals. The oldest red beds, with iron oxides, date from about 2,500 million years ago. At about this time primitive living things in the sea were beginning to use the energy of the Sun to make their food. They were the first plants. A by-product of this activity was the generation of oxygen. The oxygen gradually built up until reached its present level about 500 million years ago.

Now the atmosphere is changing again. Large-scale forest clearance cuts down the amount of oxygen produced, industry adds carbon dioxide to the atmosphere, and many processes disrupt the ozone layer. The long-term effects of these changes on climate and on living things have yet to be seen.

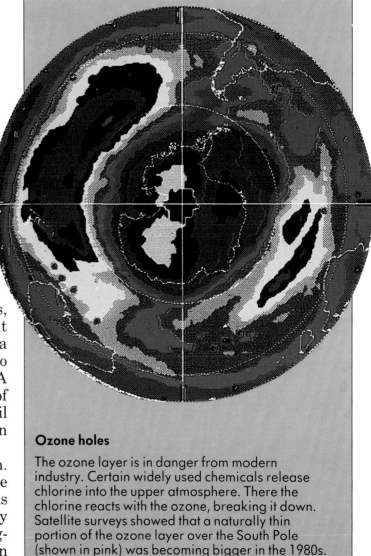

Ozone holes

The ozone layer is in danger from modern industry. Certain widely used chemicals release chlorine into the upper atmosphere. There the chlorine reacts with the ozone, breaking it down. Satellite surveys showed that a naturally thin portion of the ozone layer over the South Pole (shown in pink) was becoming bigger in the 1980s.

Weather and climate

Spot facts

● *Frozen rain can be carried up and down in a thundercloud until it forms large hailstones as big as tennis balls.*

● *Jet streams – narrow belts of high winds that circle the globe at great heights – can reach speeds of 200 km/h.*

● *Greenland acquired its name because of the plant growth produced by the warmer weather there in Viking times.*

● *Nuclear war could lead to a "nuclear winter", during which sunlight would not be able to penetrate the clouds of smoke and dust produced.*

▶ A hurricane is a violent storm of circling winds. A region of very low pressure develops over the ocean, and the air from nearby high pressure regions spirals in to balance it. This generates winds of up to 300 km/h. The centre of the hurricane moves and causes great damage wherever it passes.

There is a difference between weather and climate. In a particular geographical region, climate is the overall result of the atmospheric conditions, averaged over a long period of time. The conditions include temperature, atmospheric pressure and wind patterns. Weather, on the other hand, depends on the day-to-day variations of these conditions. Weather is important to agriculture, fishing, transport and many other human other activities. This is why meteorology – the scientific study of weather – is a very important science. Because so many people depend on them, weather reports have to be accurate.

Weather systems

The pattern of weather depends on the distribution of regions of warm air and cold air. This, in turn, depends on the distribution of low pressure areas and high pressure areas over the globe. When the Sun shines on the Earth's surface, the ground warms up. This warms the air above it. Warm air is lighter than cool air and so it rises, producing an area of low atmospheric pressure. In the cooler areas round about, the air is denser and at a higher pressure. It begins to move in towards the low pressure area. This movement produces the winds. The global wind pattern can be pictured as a reflection of the areas of high pressure and low pressure across the world.

▼ A front is the boundary between two air masses. The boundary is not stationary, but moves across the landscape. If a warm air mass is replaced by a cold one, then it is a cold front marked on a weather map by a line with teeth. A cold air mass is replaced by a warm one at a warm front represented by a line with semicircles. At a cold front the cold air wedges its way

When air rises it cools. But cool air can hold less moisture than warm air. As a result, moisture forms water droplets in a cooling air mass. These droplets form clouds and, ultimately, it rains.

As a general rule, wherever there are rising air masses there is rain. The air may be made to rise by convection currents, by winds blowing up a mountain range, or by a cold air mass pushing its way below a warm air mass where the two meet along a "front". Such fronts are found between the cold air over the North Pole and the warmer air over the tropics. They account for the unstable weather patterns in temperate Europe and North America.

beneath the warm, forcing the warm air upwards. Thunderclouds often form here as the warmer air is swept up quickly. At a warm front the warm air rises gently above the cold, producing a series of clouds at different heights. When two cold air masses catch up with each other and lift the intervening warm air, they form an occluded front .

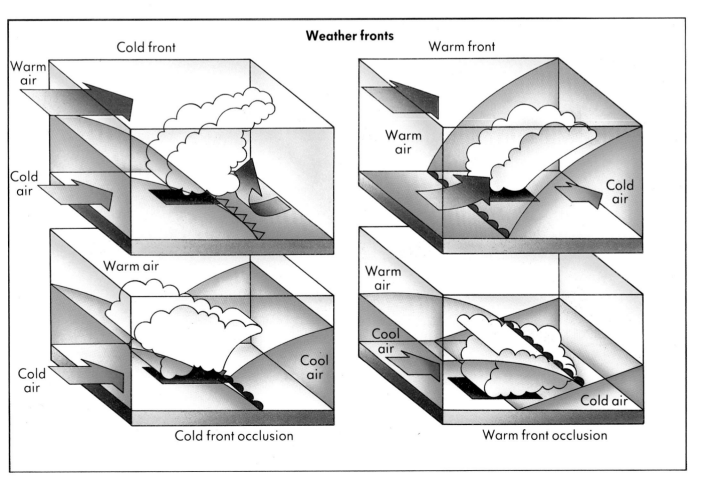

Weather fronts

Cold front — Warm front

Warm air

Cold air

Warm air

Cool air

Cold air

Cold front occlusion

Warm air

Warm air

Cool air

Cold air

Warm front occlusion

Wind

Winds are produced when cool air moves in to replace the warm air rising in a low-pressure area. The world distribution of high and low pressures determines the pattern of the usual, or prevailing, winds.

The Sun is always directly overhead somewhere between the tropics. As a result, the land areas along the Equator are among the hottest on Earth. The hot air rises there, resulting in an equatorial low-pressure belt. Air from the north and south sweeps in to equalize the pressure. This gives rise to the North-easterly Trade Winds and the South-easterly Trade Winds. (Winds are always named after the direction from which they blow.) The north-south movement of air is deflected towards the west as a result of the turning of the Earth.

The warm air that rises at the Equator spreads northwards and southwards at the top of the troposphere. There it cools before descending again in the regions of the Tropics of Cancer in the north and Capricorn in the south. Tropical high-pressure belts form there. The world's greatest deserts are found along these belts, because the descending air is dry. The air that descends may then return towards the Equator as the Trade Winds. Or it may spread towards the more temperate regions as the warm South-westerlies in the Northern Hemisphere or the North-westerlies in the Southern Hemisphere. These winds are usually referred to simply as the Westerlies.

Over the North and South Poles the cold temperatures give rise to high-pressure regions of cold air. Cold winds spread outwards from these regions and meet the Westerlies along frontal systems in the temperate regions. Where they meet, the weather patterns are unstable. These major air movements produce the basic circulation pattern of the world's winds. It is disrupted and altered by the distribution of land and sea, and by the presence of mountain ranges. All of these factors decide the various climates of the world.

▼ Damage caused by a tornado in Pennsylvania in 1965. The tremendous power of the winds is spectacularly illustrated by the damage done by storms.

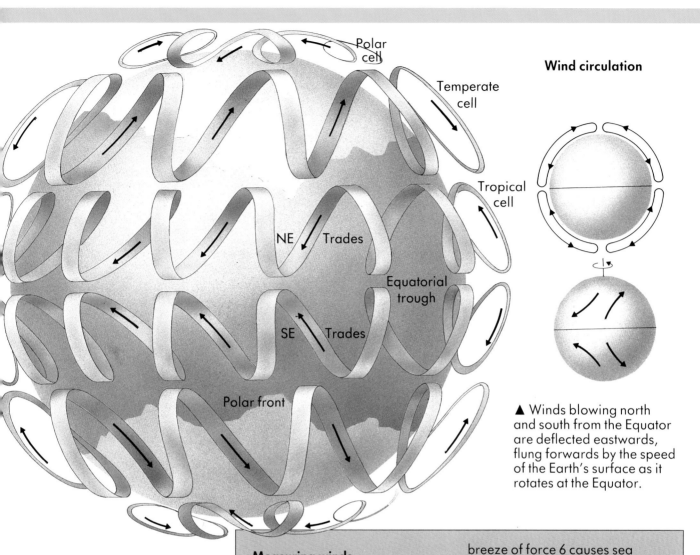

Polar cell

Temperate cell

Tropical cell

NE Trades

Equatorial trough

SE Trades

Polar front

▲ Winds blowing north and south from the Equator are deflected eastwards, flung forwards by the speed of the Earth's surface as it rotates at the Equator.

▲ The world wind pattern takes the form of a series of cells in which air rises and falls. The pattern is varied by world geography.

▼ Trees generally grow more vigorously away from the direction of the prevailing wind, giving them a characteristic leaning shape.

Measuring winds

The Beaufort scale gives wind strengths, judged by the effects they produce. Force 1 shows no air movement at all, the strong breeze of force 6 causes sea spray, and force 12 is denoted by the extensive damage caused by a hurricane. The original scale gave wind speeds in miles per hour.

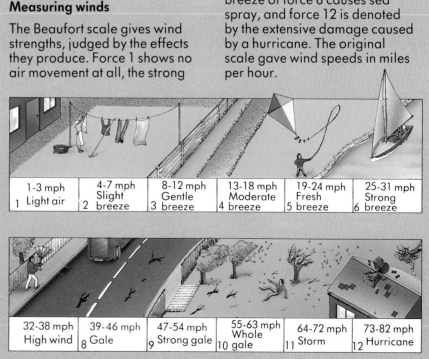

1-3 mph 1 Light air	4-7 mph 2 Slight breeze	8-12 mph 3 Gentle breeze	13-18 mph 4 Moderate breeze	19-24 mph 5 Fresh breeze	25-31 mph 6 Strong breeze
32-38 mph 7 High wind	39-46 mph 8 Gale	47-54 mph 9 Strong gale	55-63 mph 10 Whole gale	64-72 mph 11 Storm	73-82 mph 12 Hurricane

Measuring the weather

Weather forecasting had always been important to people because of the weather's influence on shipping and navigation, farming and almost every other aspect of human life. Before the development of scientific instruments, weather forecasting relied on observation. People tried to predict the weather by observing such things as wind direction, cloud types, sea colour, and so on. Then in 1643 the Italian physicist Evangelista Torricelli invented the mercury barometer, which measures atmospheric pressure. From that time on, the study of weather became a very much more exact science, now called meteorology.

Modern meteorology contains a number of branches. "Dynamical meteorology" is the branch that deals with the movements of the atmosphere. It takes the sciences of hydrodynamics – the study of movements of liquids and gases – and thermodynamics – the study of the transfer of energy through a system – and applies them to the whole vast ocean of the air.

"Micrometeorology" is the branch of meteorology that deals with more localized effects, such as the development of land and sea breezes, and the formation of valley winds.

▼ Modern meteorologists use radar to help them track the movements of storms. Radar signals are reflected by raindrops and ice particles in clouds.

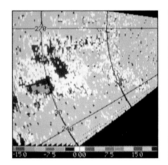
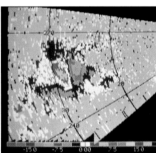

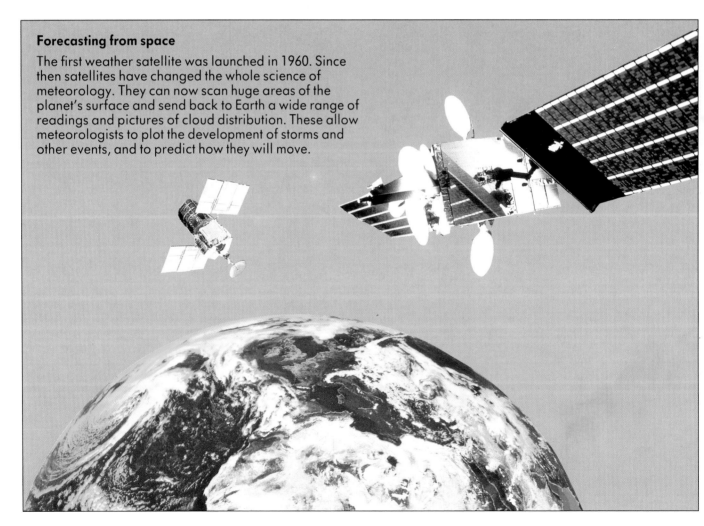

Forecasting from space

The first weather satellite was launched in 1960. Since then satellites have changed the whole science of meteorology. They can now scan huge areas of the planet's surface and send back to Earth a wide range of readings and pictures of cloud distribution. These allow meteorologists to plot the development of storms and other events, and to predict how they will move.

"Synoptic meteorology" is what we normally think of as weather forecasting. Readings of temperature, humidity, air pressure, cloud cover, wind strength and direction, and so on are taken at different places at the same time. This information is then plotted on a chart, or map, to give an overall view of the weather conditions at any particular time. Weather forecasters also use photographs of the clouds taken from orbiting satellites.

▼ A modern weather centre. Information from a large number of weather stations is fed into computers, which produce synoptic charts detailing the weather conditions over a wide area. The charts are used to make weather forecasts.

Processing data

Weather forecasting involves collecting and comparing data from many sources. Much of this is done using a computer system using CPUs (central processing units).

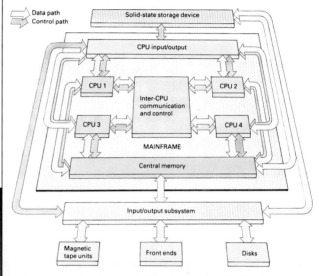

The changing climate

Over millions of years world climates change. The way they have changed can be seen by looking at rocks. In a particular area we might find beds of coal that were produced in a tropical swamp, covered by sandstones that formed in a desert. These may be covered, in turn, by mudstones deposited at the bottom of a shallow sea. Climate changes such as these take place over millions of years.

Extensive changes of climate can take place over shorter periods of time. The ice ages that began 2 million years ago – not a long time in geological terms – did not finish until 10,000 years ago. Throughout that time the world's climate varied widely. At times much of the Northern Hemisphere was choked with ice caps and glaciers. Then a few thousand years later the climates were warmer than they are now. A few thousand years later still the glaciers swept southwards again.

Even in historical times there have been major changes in the climate. On the Tassili Plateau in the middle of the Sahara Desert, there are old rock paintings showing grassland animals. They must have been painted when the local climate was much moister than it is now. Trees still grow nearby. They have immensely long roots which extract water from

▲ The Mexican volcano El Chichon erupted in 1982, sending 16 million tonnes of dust into the atmosphere. The result was an enormous dust veil that absorbed some of the sunlight, leading to a measurable lowering of the Earth's surface temperatures.

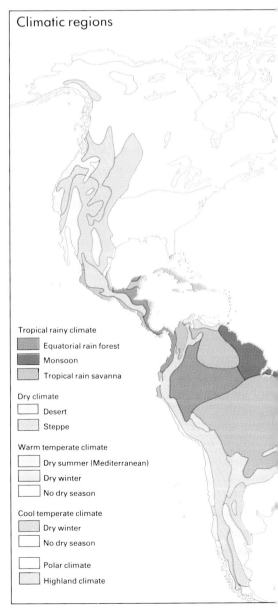

Climatic regions

Tropical rainy climate

- Equatorial rain forest
- Monsoon
- Tropical rain savanna

Dry climate

- Desert
- Steppe

Warm temperate climate

- Dry summer (Mediterranean)
- Dry winter
- No dry season

Cool temperate climate

- Dry winter
- No dry season

- Polar climate
- Highland climate

deep rocks. These trees could not have started growing unless there was water on the surface. Europe suffered a "Little Ice Age" between the 13th and 14th centuries, when climates were very much colder than they are now. In winter, fairs were regularly held on the frozen River Thames, which be impossible nowadays because it does not get cold enough.

The changes in climate through geological time, as revealed by the different rocks, can be explained by the drifting of the continents from one climatic region to another. More recent changes are due to shorter-term events. Volcanic eruptions can throw up dust and gases such as sulphur dioxide high into the atmosphere. There they can block out sunlight and lower the temperatures on the Earth's surface. A noticeable cooling in the 1960s coincided with increasing volcanic activity across the globe.

Another influence may be a fluctuation in the energy output of the Sun itself. Old astronomical records show that the Sun does, indeed, change in size and energy output from time to time. These changes alter the climate.

▼ The Earth can be divided into a number of distinct climatic zones. Changing conditions may mean that maps like this will be inaccurate within a few decades.

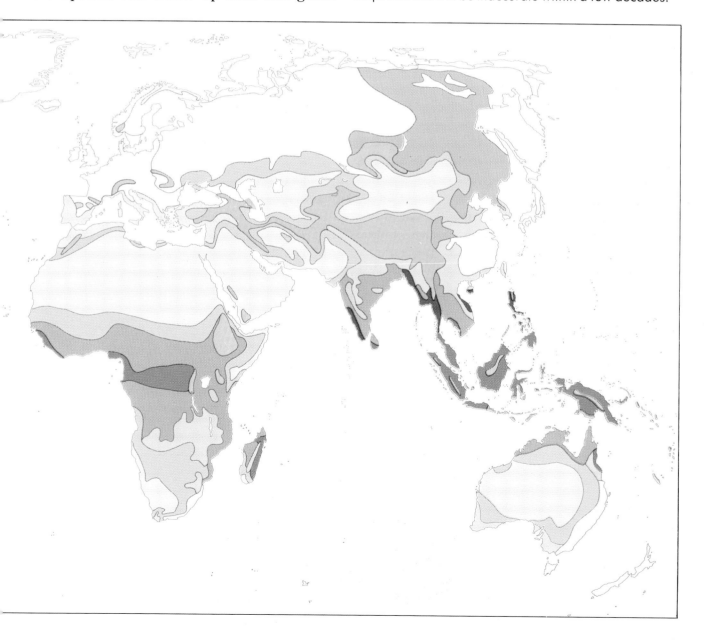

Climates of the world

Spot facts

- *The biggest daily range of temperature recorded was from 52°C to −2°C in the Sahara Desert.*

- *The world's most disastrous flood was in 1877 when the Hwang-ho River in China burst its banks, killing 900,000 people.*

- *Temperatures in Antarctica may fall as low as −85°C.*

- *The hottest place in the world is Death Valley, California, with extremely high temperatures of up to 57°C.*

The Sun's heating effect is stronger at the Equator than at the poles. This produces different surface temperatures over the face of the Earth. It also produces areas of high and low atmospheric pressure, and these generate the pattern of prevailing winds. The distribution of land and sea, the patchwork of the continents and the sweep of the mountain ranges modify the pattern produced. The result is a range of different climates and environmental conditions in different parts of the world. Some are bitterly cold; others are very hot.

▶ Equatorial rain forests flourish because the heat and humidity found along the Equator are ideal for vigorous plant growth. The trees are homes for thousands of different species of animals.

Rain forest climate

The Sun is almost overhead at the Equator. Its rays come vertically downwards, cutting straight through the atmosphere and concentrating their energy on small areas of ground. The air becomes very hot and it rises, producing a belt of low pressure along the Equator. This draws in the Trade Winds from the north-east and south-east. The winds usually travel over oceans and so their air is very moist. When the air reaches the low-pressure areas, it begins to rise. Clouds form and drop their water on the land beneath as daily torrential downpours.

This vigorous circulation of water produces vast networks of streams flowing into the greatest rivers of the world. The Amazon, the Zaire and the Mekong all flow close to the Equator. The humid lowland plains they flow through have a hothouse atmosphere. Plants grow in profusion and produce the tropical rain forest. The conditions are so good for plant life that many thousands of different species can exist in a few square kilometres. They produce trees up to 70 m tall, all growing past each other to reach the sunlight.

Smaller plants called epiphytes grow on the branches, and others in the form of creepers climb up the trunks to reach the light. The intertwined and entangled mass of branches, leaves and creepers forms a green canopy over the whole forest. The tallest trees, the emergents, reach through the canopy into the air above. The forest floor is dark and hot, and few plants grow except where a fallen tree leaves space for the Sun to shine in. Along the river banks the crowns of branches and leaves come right down to ground level.

The vast range of plant types supports a variety of animals as well. Most of these stay among the sunlit branches, although some live in the darkness below.

◄ The gibbon of south-eastern Asia is the most agile of tree-dwelling animals and it eats fruit. The wide variety of plants in the tropical forest has led to the evolution of a range of animals to feed on them.

▼ The several species of sloth from South America are among the slowest-moving of the tree-dwelling mammals. They hang upside-down and live on a diet of leaves.

Grasslands

Grasslands develop naturally in regions where the climate is generally dry but has distinct moist seasons. Grasses can weather long periods of drought because of their underground stems. The leaves and heads may die off in dry weather, but they can grow again from the underground part of the plant. Trees generally do not thrive in such conditions, and the typical landscape is one of wide open plains with very few trees.

The tropical grasslands occur in two bands north and south of the Equator. They lie between the central belt of equatorial rain forest and the two belts of desert along the tropics. As the Earth moves round in its orbit and the Sun appears to move north and south in the sky between summer and winter, the rainy conditions that produce the tropical forest move north and south too. The regions that lie between the forest and desert belts get both types of climate. They have the forest weather at one part of the year, and the desert weather at another. The resulting vegetation is known as tropical grasslands. They can be traced from one continent to another, but they are most prominent in Africa.

▼ The grasslands that we see in moist temperate regions tend not to be natural. Throughout civilization communities have chopped down trees and cut clearings for fields. These take on the appearance of grasslands because the important cereal crops are themselves grasses.

▶ Grassland animals, such as these pronghorn antelopes, have very strong teeth for chewing grass, and complex digestive systems for digesting it. They also have long legs and are built for speed. The best method of defence from predators is to run away.

Temperate grasslands are found deep within continents, usually bordering on cool desert areas. The prairies of North America and the steppes of Asia are the northern examples. In the south, the pampas of South America are partly temperate and partly tropical.

Grassland animals are highly specialized, because grass is a difficult food to digest. The development of grasslands 50 million years ago allowed grazing animals, such as horses, antelopes and cattle, to evolve. In turn, grazing stimulates fresh growth and the animal dung keeps the ground fertilized.

◄ Elephants are not typical of the grassland animals. They are slow-moving, and rather than feed on grass they tend to eat the shoots and leaves of the few bushes and trees that grow there.

▲ The South American rheas, the African ostrich and the Australian emu share the same grassland lifestyle. Flightless birds are typical of grasslands. Their long legs enable them to run quickly over the plains.

◄ The long face of the zebra is typical of a grassland animal. Its mouth can be down munching the grass but its eyes are still quite high and looking about. When zebras graze in herds, there are always one or two animals looking out for danger.

Deciduous and boreal forest

Deciduous trees are those that lose their leaves in winter and grow new ones each spring. The deciduous woodlands are found in the temperate regions of the Earth, mostly in the Northern Hemisphere. The temperate zone is a broad band which, at times, is subjected to the cold wind moving away from the poles. At other times, it is exposed to the warm Westerlies. As a result, the climate is a mild one compared to other climates of the world. It is generally moist and does not have extremes of heat or cold.

This zone has particularly favourable places for people to live and grow crops. Over the centuries, much of the original deciduous forest has cleared away for cities and farms. The common large trees of these woodlands are broad-leaved types, such as oaks, ashes, beeches and willows. Smaller trees growing beneath them include maples and birches. At a lower level still grow the bushes of dogwoods, hollies and hawthorns, and there is usually a thick undergrowth of flowering plants.

To the north of the belt of deciduous woodland lies the largest stretch of uninterrupted forest in the world. The great coniferous boreal forest stretches from Scandinavia eastwards across northern Europe and Asia, then across Alaska and Canada. There the prevailing weather is brought by the cold air masses that blow in from the far north.

The growing season is only three or four months long, and during the lengthy winter all the moisture is locked in ice and snow. The coniferous trees can withstand these conditions.

▶ Deer are the typical animals of deciduous woodland. They eat a number of different foods, including leaves and young shoots from the trees and the undergrowth.

▼ A deciduous woodland has several different kinds trees, with a spread of bushes and an undergrowth of many small flowering plants.

The needle-shaped leaves of coniferous trees reduce the rate at which water is given off through them. The leaves stay on the tree all year round, so that they are ready as soon as the growing season begins. The trees' conical shape allows snow to slide off easily.

Although coniferous trees are particularly well adapted for the cold conditions, they are found in more temperate regions as well. The deciduous woodlands rarely consist of only deciduous trees but usually have conifers among them – giving a "mixed woodland".

▲ There are fewer animals and birds in coniferous forests than in deciduous woodlands, and they tend to be quite specialized feeders. Crossbills (1), for example, eat only seed cones. The coniferous forests of Canada (2) are home to the beaver – a creature that can alter its habitat. Beaver colonies can fell trees and dam rivers, holding back lakes in which they build their lodges. The blunt face of the beaver (3) hides a massive set of chisel-like incisor teeth. It uses these to fell the trees, and groups of about 12 cooperate in building the dams and lodges.

Mountain climate

Conditions change as we climb a high mountain. The higher we go, the thinner the air becomes. The sky also gets bluer and the Sun's rays become hotter. There is a change in climate between the mountain's base and its summit. The difference can be similar to the difference between the climate at the Equator and at the North Pole or South Pole.

At the base of an equatorial mountain, such as Mount Kenya or Mount Kilimanjaro in eastern Africa, there may be tropical forest or tropical grassland. Higher up the temperature falls, and the climate becomes moister because of rain falling from the rising clouds. At about 1,500 m the original tropical conditions give way to those of moist temperate forests.

Above about 2,400 m there is less rainfall and the forest gives way to scrub. Grasses become the main plants. In the African and Asian mountains, bamboo is the most common.

The bamboo and scrub give way at a height of about 3,000 m to open moorland, with tussocks of coarse grasses and heathers. Up there the conditions are too harsh for trees to grow, and the landscape is similar to that of the tundra regions of the far north.

Above the tree-line

Just as the tundra in the north gives way to the ice-caps of the North Pole, so the moorland of the mountain gives way to the glaciers and snow-covered crags of the mountain summit. On top of the African mountains there are permanent snowfields and glaciers, even though they lie near the Equator.

Most mountain slopes are gentle, especially among the foothills. Changes in climate usually take place over quite large distances. But in the Himalayas, the gorge of the River Brahmaputra is so narrow and steep that conditions change from tropical forest to snow and ice within a kilometre or two.

▶ Big horn sheep in Alaska. The change in climate between the base of a mountain and its summit is accompanied by a change in plant and animal life. Typical forest animals such as pigs and deer give way to more specialized creatures on the higher slopes. In Asia, giant pandas live at this level, and in Africa there are mountain gorillas. Sure-footed mountain goats and ibexes live on the sparse grazing of the higher reaches.

Ice

Tundra

Scrub

Cloud forest

Rainforest

Arid ground

Deserts and polar climates

Plants need a certain minimum amount of water to survive. Very few plants can grow in particularly dry regions, where there is very little rainfall or all the moisture is locked up as ice. The barren landscape that results is known as a desert.

Hot deserts are the kind that usually come to mind when we think of a desert. There are several types of hot deserts. Tropical deserts lie in two belts along the Tropics of Cancer and Capricorn. Hot air that has risen and released its moisture as rain over the low-pressure equatorial belt now descends over the tropics. This dry air forms high-pressure belts and no moist winds blow over these areas. The great deserts of the Sahara and Arabia lie in this zone in the north. In the south there are the Kalahari in Africa and the Gibson in Australia.

Continental deserts exist in places that are so far from the sea that the moist winds just cannot reach them. The Gobi Desert in central Asia is a typical example.

Finally there is the rain shadow desert, which is found on the lee side of mountain ranges (the side away from the wind). Winds from the ocean lose all their moisture in rain as they rise up the seaward mountain slopes, leaving only dry air to pass over to the other side. California's Death Valley is the most famous rain shadow desert.

Hot deserts are usually surrounded by zones of semidesert, in which only specialized types of plants can grow. This is also true of the cold deserts. Beyond the northern reaches of the great coniferous forests there is a region in which the climate is too harsh for trees. It is an area of permanently frozen subsoil with a vegetation of coarse grasses, heathers and

▲ Cactus plants have a thick fleshy stem that holds water, a leathery waterproof skin to keep the moisture in, and spines to protect them from damage by animals. All these features enable them to survive in harsh desert conditions.

◄ Death Valley in California is the hottest place on Earth. For most of the year it is totally dry. But when the rains do come they occur as torrential downpours with several centimetres falling in a day. Immediately afterwards the desert blooms with all kinds of plants before it returns to barrenness for the remainder of the year.

other small herbaceous plants. It is called the tundra where it occurs in Europe and Asia, or the muskeg in Canada.

Islands close to the North Pole and the continent of Antarctica at the South Pole can be regarded as true deserts. As a result of the Earth's tilt, the Sun shines there for only part of the year, and when it does its rays slant through thick layers of atmosphere. Because of the permanently low temperatures water is always frozen and useless to living things.

▼ The icy lands of the far north are barren enough to be considered as deserts. However, the sea supports a great deal of life. Algae grow in the waters, and are eaten by fish. The fish are food for seals which are, in turn, hunted by polar bears. Birds, such as gulls, act as scavengers.

▲ Small cushion-like plants grow all over the tundra. Their compact shape gives them protection against the severe weather.

▶ Reindeer graze on the tundra vegetation in summer, but migrate southwards to the forest in winter.

Glossary

acid rain Rain that contains so much dissolved impurity that it gives an acid reaction. The impurities are usually due to industrial smoke, and the acidity can cause considerable damage to trees and lakes.

anaerobic Referring to a reaction that takes place without oxygen.

aphelion The point in a planet's orbit at which it is closest to the Sun.

atmosphere The envelope of gas that surrounds a planet. The Earth's atmosphere consists of nitrogen, oxygen and small proportions of other gases.

aurora A light display in the sky caused by particles from the Sun's radiation reacting with the Earth's magnetic field. Usually called the Aurora Borealis, or Northern Lights, in the Northern Hemisphere, and the Aurora Australis, or Southern Lights, in the Southern Hemisphere.

barometer An instrument for measuring atmospheric pressure.

biochemistry The chemical reactions that take place inside a living body.

climate The sum of the atmospheric conditions at a particular place averaged out over a long period of time.

convection A current that is formed as warm fluid, being lighter than its surroundings, rises. At the same time cooler fluid descends.

Coriolis effect An effect caused by the Earth's rotation, whereby anything moving towards the Equator is deflected to the west, and anything moving away from the Equator is deflected to the east.

cumulus A cloud with a heaped and hummocky-shaped appearance.

deciduous A term that describes a type of tree. A deciduous tree is one that loses its leaves in winter.

delta A structure of sandbanks, islands and channels formed at the mouth of a river, where tides and currents cannot carry away the river's sediment.

ecosystem A community of organisms all interacting with one another.

environment The sum total of conditions under which an organism lives. These conditions include such things as the climate, the soil, the water and the other organisms present.

erosion The process whereby the rocks and soils of the surface of the Earth are broken down by the action of the weather, by streams, by glaciers or by human interference.

evolve Of a living organism, to change from generation to generation in response to changing conditions, producing new species.

fossil The remains or trace of a once-living organism preserved in the rocks.

front In meteorology, the boundary between two air masses of different temperatures. Fronts are usually associated with unstable weather.

gravity A force of attraction between objects as a result their mass. The most obvious result of this is that objects fall to Earth.

greenhouse effect A condition of the atmosphere in which the gases present will allow radiation from the Sun to reach the Earth's surface, but will not allow the reradiated heat from the Earth's surface to escape, thereby increasing the temperature. The artificial increase of such gases as carbon dioxide and water vapour from industry is a current cause.

groundwater Water that is held in the rocks and soil of the Earth.

gyre A large circular motion of seawater caused by ocean currents and Coriolis effect. A gyre typically occupies half an ocean.

iceberg A mass of ice floating in the sea, broken from a glacier or an ice flow.

invertebrate An animal with no backbone. Effectively this is any animal that is not a fish, amphibian, reptile, bird or mammal.

irrigation Bringing water to a dry landscape to enable plants to grow.

meander A loop in a river's course, typical of river's old age.

meteorite A body of rock or particle of dust from space that reaches the ground.

meteorology The study of the movement of the atmosphere and the weather.

monsoon A seasonal effect in the countries bordering the north Indian Ocean, in which cold winds blow outwards from the Asian continent in the cooler times of the year, and warm, wet winds blow inwards in the warmer times.

nebula A cloud of gas and dust in space.

oasis A moist, fertile spot in a desert area.

observatory An establishment where natural phenomenon, such as the stars, earthquakes or the weather, are studied.

oceanography The study of the oceans.

ocean ridge An elevated part of the ocean bed that winds throughout the oceans of the world. It represents the tectonic plate boundary, where new material is welling up from the Earth's interior and forming new plates.

ocean trench An elongated deep section of the ocean floor, usually found close to mountainous continents or island arcs. It represents a tectonic plate boundary, where one old plate is being dragged down beneath another.

oceanic zone The area of open sea lying beyond the edge of the continental shelf and where the depth is greater than 200 metres.

ooze Deep ocean sediment formed from the remains of living creatures.

orbit The path in space of one body around another, as the Moon around the Earth. The forward momentum of the first body just balances the gravitational effect of the second, so that the one falls around the other without touching it.

organic Referring to the chemistry of living things.

ox-bow A curved lake left behind as a meander is cut off when a river changes its course.

ozone A type of oxygen that contains three atoms of oxygen in its molecules instead of the usual two.

ozone layer A layer in the atmosphere where ozone is being generated. This acts as a shield against ultraviolet solar radiation. Deterioration of the ozone layer, through pollution of the atmosphere, will allow more harmful radiation to reach the Earth's surface.

perihelion The point in a planet's orbit at which it is farthest from the Sun.

planet A large body in orbit around the Sun or another star.

polarized light Light in which the waves vibrate in one plane only. This can be the result of reflection of the light from a flat surface, or of the light's passage through a polarizing filter. Polarized light can be blocked by filters that are polarized at right angles to the beam. Certain minerals distort polarized light to produce colours that can be used to identify them.

pollution The poisoning of an environment by unwanted substances.

prevailing wind A wind that blows from a particular direction for most of the time.

reef A rocky outcrop that produces a shallow area out at sea. The term is usually reserved for the structures built by the action of corals.

salinity The measure of the amount of substance dissolved in seawater, that is its saltiness.

seafloor spreading The phenomenon whereby the ocean floor is observed to become older farther away from the ocean ridges. The discovery was made in the 1960s and is now covered by the all-embracing concept of plate tectonics.

sediment Any loose material deposited in layers by the action of water or wind.

soil A loose covering of natural material, consisting of broken-down rocky material mixed with decomposing plant matter.

Solar System The group of bodies in space comprising the Sun, the planets, all their moons and an unknown number of rocky bodies and comets, all under the gravitational influence of the Sun.

stratus A cloud with a layered appearance.

subduction zone A line along which one tectonic plate is being destroyed beneath another. Subduction zones are usually marked by the presence of ocean trenches.

subsoil The layer of soil between the topsoil and the bedrock, containing little organic matter.

survey To study a tract of land by making measurements and investigating its features.

technology The application of science to industry, research, commerce, and other fields of human endeavour.

tornado A rapidly spinning column of air, caused by an intense convection current usually along a front. Sometimes called a whirlwind.

Trade Winds Prevailing winds that blow towards the Equator from the north-east and the south-east. So called because they were vital to the trade routes before the advent of powered ships.

tropic One of the two lines of latitude that mark the boundaries of the zone in which the Sun is overhead sometime during the year. The tropic of Cancer is 23½° N. The tropic of Capricorn is 23½° S.

troposphere The lowest layer of the Earth's atmosphere, up to a height of about 11 km. All weather phenomena occur and all life exists within this layer. The upper boundary is irregular, being higher in the tropics than at the poles.

tundra The landscape of the far north, characterized by a lack of trees and a very wet appearance in the summer. The significant feature is the permafrost – a layer of permanently frozen subsoil that prevents the summer meltwater from draining away.

typhoon The term used in the Far East for a hurricane.

ultraviolet Any wavelength of light that is too short to be seen by the naked eye.

weather The daily changing climatic conditions at any place on the Earth's surface.

weathering Erosion caused by the influence of weather conditions. Such conditions include rain, freezing water, sandblasting by wind, heating by the Sun, or chemical decomposition by acids dissolved in rainwater.

Index

Further Reading

Conserving the Atmosphere by John Baines (Wayland, 1990)
The Oceans by Martin Bramwell (Franklin Watts, 1984)
Weather by A. Ganeri (Usborne, 1988)
Into the Air by Robin Kerrod (Macdonald, 1986)
Seas and Oceans by David Lambert (Wayland, 1989)
The Ocean Floor by Keith Lye (Wayland, 1990)
Weather and Climate by John Mason (Wayland, 1988)
Waves, Tides and Currents by Daniel Rogers (Wayland, 1990)
Storm by A. B. C. Whipple (Time-Life, 1982)
The Science of the Earth by Tom Williamson (Macmillan, 1984)
The Weather by Francis Wilson (Purnell, 1988)